THE USBORNE INTERNET-LINKED
FIRST THOUSAND WORDS
IN PORTUGUESE

With Internet-linked pronunciation guide

Heather Amery

Illustrated by Stephen Cartwright

Edited by Mairi Mackinnon

Portuguese language consultants: Valéria Correll and Octávio Gameiro

Usborne Quicklinks: notes for parents and guardians

Please ensure that your children read and follow the internet safety
guidelines displayed on the Usborne Quicklinks Website.

The links in Usborne Quicklinks are regularly reviewed and updated.
However, the content of a website may change at any time, and Usborne
Publishing is not responsible for the content on any website other than its
own. We recommend that children are supervised while on the internet,
that they do not use internet chat rooms and that you use internet filtering
software to block unsuitable material. For more information, see the
Net Help area on the Usborne Quicklinks Website.

On every double page with pictures, there is a little
yellow duck to look for. Can you find it?

About this book

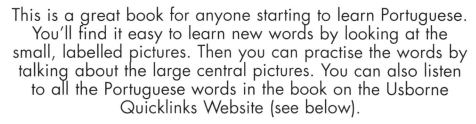

This is a great book for anyone starting to learn Portuguese. You'll find it easy to learn new words by looking at the small, labelled pictures. Then you can practise the words by talking about the large central pictures. You can also listen to all the Portuguese words in the book on the Usborne Quicklinks Website (see below).

The Portuguese language

Portuguese is spoken both in Portugal and in Brazil. This book uses European Portuguese. Some words are different in Brazilian Portuguese, and the Brazilian accent is slightly different – rather like the differences between British and American English – but if you use this book to talk to a Brazilian Portuguese speaker, they will understand you perfectly well.

Masculine and feminine words

When you look at the Portuguese words for things such as "table" or "man", you will see that they have **o** or **a** in front of them. This is because all Portuguese words for people and things are either masculine or feminine. The word for "the" is **o** in front of a masculine word, and **a** in front of a feminine word. For plurals (more than one), you use **os** and **as**.

Reading Portuguese words

Some Portuguese words have accents – signs that are written over or under the letter. Some accents tell you to stress the letter (make it sound more strongly). Others, particularly **ã**, **ç** and **õ**, change the sound of the letter. Find out more about how to pronounce the words on pages 56-64.

Hear the words on the internet

You can listen to all the words in this book, read by a native Portuguese speaker, on the Usborne Quicklinks Website. Just go to **www.usborne-quicklinks.com** and enter the keywords **1000 portuguese**. There you can:
- listen to the first thousand words in Portuguese
- find links to other useful websites about Portugal and Brazil and the Portuguese language.

Your computer needs a sound card (almost all computers have these) and may also need a small program, called an audio player, such as RealPlayer® or Windows® Media Player. If you don't already have a copy, you can download one from the Usborne Quicklinks Website.

A casa

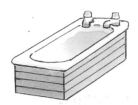
a banheira

o sabonete

a torneira

o papel higiénico

a escova de dentes

a água

a sanita

a esponja

o lavatório

o chuveiro

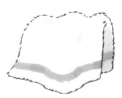
a toalha

a cama

A casa de banho

A sala de estar

a pasta de dentes

o rádio

a almofada

o CD

a alcatifa

o sofá

 a cadeira

 o edredão

 o pente

 o lençol

 o tapete

 o guarda-roupa

O quarto

 a almofada

 a cómoda

 o espelho

 a escova

 o candeeiro

A entrada

 os cartazes

 o cabide

 o telefone

 o aquecedor

 a cassete de vídeo

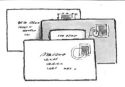 o jornal

 a mesa

 as cartas

as escadas

5

A cozinha

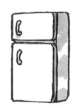

o frigorífico

os copos

o relógio

o banco

as colheres

o interruptor

o detergente

a chave

a porta

o aspirador

o lava-louça

as caçarolas

os garfos

o avental

a tábua de
passar a ferro

o lixo

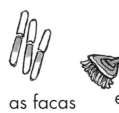
a chaleira

as facas

a esfregona

o pano
do pó

os azulejos

a vassoura

a máquina de
lavar roupa

a pá do lixo

a gaveta

os pires

a frigideira

o fogão

as
colheres de pau

os pratos

o ferro-de-engomar

o armário

o pano
de cozinha

as
chávenas

a caixa de
fósforos

a escova

as taças

O jardim

o carrinho de mão

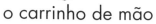
a colmeia

o caracol

os tijolos

o pombo

a pá

a joaninha

o caixote do lixo

as sementes

o barracão

o regador

a minhoca

as flores

o aspersor de rega

a enxada

a vespa

a abelha

a pá

o osso

a sebe

a forquilha

o cortador de relva

o caminho

as folhas

a árvore

o fumo

a lagarta

o ancinho

o ninho

os paus

a relva

o carrinho de bebé

a escada

a fogueira

a mangueira

a estufa

9

A oficina

os parafusos

o
torno de bancada

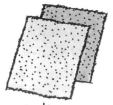
a lixa

a broca

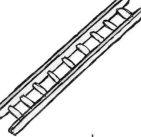
a escada

a serra

a serradura

o calendário

a caixa de
ferramentas

a chave de
parafusos

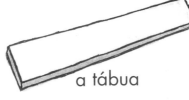
a tábua

as aparas
de madeira

o canivete

10

as tachas

a aranha

os parafusos
de porca

as porcas

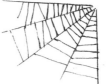
a teia de aranha

o barril

a mosca

o machado

a fita métrica

o martelo

a lima

a lata de tinta

a plaina

os pedaços
de madeira

os pregos

a bancada

os boiões

11

A rua

a loja

o buraco

o café

a ambulância

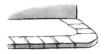
o passeio

a antena de televisão

a chaminé

o telhado

a escavadora

o hotel

o autocarro

o homem

o carro da polícia

os canos

o martelo pneumático

a escola

o recreio

 o táxi

 a passadeira de peões

 a fábrica

 o camião

 o semáforo

o cinema

 a carrinha

 o cilindro

 o reboque

 a casa

 o mercado

 os degraus

 a moto

 o prédio

 a bicicleta

 o carro dos bombeiros

 o polícia

 o carro

a mulher

 o candeeiro de rua

13

A loja de brinquedos

o comboio

os dados

a flauta

o robot

os tambores

o colar

a máquina fotográfica

as contas

as bonecas

a guitarra

o anel

a casa de bonecas

a harmónica

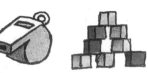
o apito   os cubos

o castelo

o submarino

a trombeta

as flecha

o arco

o pára-quedas

o barco à vela

as pinturas para a cara

o cilindro

as máscaras

o carro de corrida

o cavalo de baloiço

o mealheiro

os berlindes

as marionetas

o piano

os astronautas

a grua

a plasticina

a espingarda

os soldadinhos de chumbo

as aguarelas

o foguetão

15

os baloiços

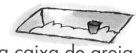
a caixa de areia

o piquenique

o papagaio de papel

o gelado

o cão

o portão

o caminho

a rã

O parque

o banco de jardim

o escorrega

os girinos

o lago

os patins

o arbusto

 o bebé

 o skate

a terra

 a cadeira de bebé

 o sobe e desce

 as crianças

 o triciclo

 os pássaros

 a cerca

 a bola

 o barco à vela

 o barbante

 a poça de água

 os patinhos

 a corda de saltar

 as árvores

o canteiro

os cisnes

a trela

os patos

O jardim zoológico

a asa

a águia

o hipopótamo

o panda

as patas

o gorila

o canguru

o morcego

o macaco

o icebergue

o pinguim

a cauda

o lobo

o urso

as penas

o crocodilo

o pelicano

o golfinho

a avestruz

o leão

os filhotes de leão

a girafa

as armações

o veado

o dromedário

a foca

a tartaruga

o elefante

a tromba

o urso polar

o rinoceronte

o bisonte

o castor

a cabra

a zebra

a serpente

o tubarão

a baleia

o tigre

o leopardo

19

As viagens

os carris

a locomotiva

os amortecedores

as carruagens

o maquinista

o comboio de mercadorias

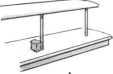
o cais

a revisora

a mala

a máquina de bilhetes

o helicóptero

A estação de comboio

A estação de serviço

os sinais

a mochila

os faróis

o motor

a roda

a bateria

o avião

a hospedeira

a pista de aterragem

O aeroporto

a torre
de controlo

o comissário
de bordo

o piloto

a lavagem
automática

o porta-bagagens

a gasolina

o reboque

a bomba de
gasolina

LAVAGEM AUTOMÁTICA

o camião-cisterna

a chave-
inglesa

o pneu

o capô

o óleo

21

O campo

o moinho
de vento

o balão

a borboleta

o lagarto

as pedras

a raposa

o regato

o poste
sinalizador

o ouriço-cacheiro

a montanha

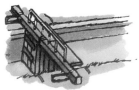

a comporta

o esquilo

a floresta

o texugo

o rio

a estrada

as tendas de campismo

o canal

a lenha

a aldeia

a borboleta nocturna

a ponte

a barcaça

a cascata

o mocho

o túnel

as raposinhas

a toupeira

o pescador

os rochedos

o sapo

o comboio

a caravana

a colina

A quinta

a meda de feno

o cão pastor

os patos

os cordeiros

o charco

os pintainhos

o palheiro

a pocilga

o touro

os patinhos

o galinheiro

o tractor

o galo

os gansos

o camião-cisterna

o celeiro

a lama

a carroça

24

 o lavrador

o campo

 as galinhas

 o bezerro

a cerca

 a sela

 o estábulo

 a vaca

o arado

 o pomar

 a cavalariça

os leitões

 a pastora

 os perus

 o espantalho

 a quinta

 o feno

as ovelhas

os fardos de palha

 o cavalo

 os porcos

A praia

o barco à vela

o mar

o remo

o farol

a pá

o balde

a estrela-do-mar

o castelo de areia

o guarda-sol

o guarda-sol

a bandeira

o marinheiro

a concha

o caranguejo

a gaivota

a ilha

o barco a motor

o esqui aquático

26

as ondas

o chapéu
de palha

o penhasco

o navio

a canoa

a corda

os seixos

as algas

a rede

o remo
de canoa

a traineira

as barbatanas

o burro

o peixe

o fato
de banho

o petroleiro

a praia

o barco a remos

a cadeira
de praia

A escola

a tesoura

as contas

a borracha

a régua

as fotografias

os marcadores

as tachas

as tintas

o menino

o lápis

o quadro

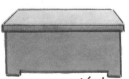
a secretária

os livros

a caneta

a cola

o giz

o desenho

o cesto de papéis

a professora

a caixa

o mapa

o pincel

o tecto

a parede

o chão

o caderno

a b c d e f
g h i j k l m n
o p q r s t u
v w x y z

o abecedário

o distintivo

o aquário

o papel

a persiana

o puxador

a planta

o globo terrestre

a menina

os lápis de cera

o candeeiro

o quadro preto

O hospital

o enfermeiro

o algodão

o medicamento

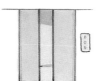
o elevador

o roupão

as muletas

os comprimidos

o tabuleiro

o relógio

o termómetro

a cortina

o urso de peluche

a maçã

o gesso

a ligadura

a cadeira de rodas

o puzzle

a médica

a seringa

30

O consultório

as pantufas

o computador

o penso-rápido

a banana

as uvas

o cesto

os brinquedos

a pêra

os cartões
ilustrados

a fralda

a bengala

a televisão

a camisa
de dormir

o pijama

a laranja

os lenços
de papel

a revista

a sala de
espera

A festa

o balão

o chocolate

o rebuçado

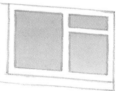

a janela

os foguetes

o laço

o bolo

as prendas

a palhinha

a vela

a grinalda de papel

os brinquedos

a tangerina

o salame

a cassete

a salsicha

as batatas fritas

os disfarces

a cereja

o sumo

a framboesa

o morango

a lâmpada

a sanduíche

a manteiga

a bolacha

o queijo

o pão

a toalha de mesa

33

O supermercado

a toranja

a cenoura

a couve-flor

o alho-francês

o cogumelo

o pepino

o limão

o aipo

o alperce

o melão

o saco

QUEIJO

FRUTAS E LEGUMES

a cebola

a couve

o pêssego

a alface

as ervilhas

o tomate

os ovos

 a ameixa

 a farinha

 a balança

 os boiões

 a carne

 o ananás

 o iogurte

 o cesto

 as garrafas

 a mala

 o porta-moedas

 o dinheiro

 as latas de conserva

 o carrinho de compras

 as batatas

 os espinafres

o feijão verde

 a caixa

 a abóbora

35

Os alimentos

o almoço

o pequeno-almoço

o ovo quente

as torradas

a compota

o café

o ovo estrelado

as natas

os cereais

o chocolate quente

o leite

o açúcar

o mel

a pimenta

o sal

o bule

o chá

as panquecas

os pãezinhos

o jantar

o presunto

a sopa

a omeleta

os pauzinhos

a salada

o hambúrger

o frango

o arroz

o molho de tomate

o esparguete

o puré de batata

a pizza

as batatas fritas

as sobremesas

Eu

a cabeça

o cabelo

a cara

o braço

o cotovelo

o estômago

os dedos do pé

o pé

a perna

o joelho

a sobrancelha

o olho

o nariz

a bochecha

a boca

os lábios

os dentes

a língua

o queixo

as orelhas

o pescoço

os ombros

o peito

as costas

o rabinho

a mão

o polegar

os dedos

A roupa

as meias

as cuecas

a camisola interior

as calças

as calças de ganga

a T-shirt

a saia

a camisa

a gravata

os calções

as meias-calças

o vestido

o pulôver

a camisola

o casaco de malha

o cachecol

o lenço

os sapatos de ténis

os sapatos

as sandálias

as botas

as luvas

os bolsos

o cinto

a fivela

o fecho de correr

o atacador

o botão

a casa do botão

o casaco

o blusão

o boné

o chapéu

As profissões

o actor   a actriz

o cozinheiro-chefe

o bailarino   a bailarina

o cantor

a cantora

o astronauta

o talhante

o polícia

a mulher-polícia

o carpinteiro

o bombeiro

a pintora

o juiz

o mecânico

a mecânica

40

o cabeleireiro

a camionista

o motorista de autocarro

a dentista

o mergulhador

o empregado

a empregada

o carteiro

o pintor

a padeira

A família

o filho
o irmão

a filha
a irmã

a mãe
a esposa

o pai
o marido

a tia

o tio

o primo

o avô

a avó

As acções

sorrir

chorar

pensar

escutar

rir

apanhar

lançar

partir

pintar

escrever

rachar

cortar

comer

falar

cavar

carregar

beber

colar

saltar

dançar

lavar-se

fazer malha

gatinhar

42

jogar

ver

trepar

lutar

dormir

pegar

coser

saltar à corda

esperar

cozinhar

esconder-se

ler

comprar

empurrar

varrer

cantar

colher

soprar

puxar

cair

andar

correr

estar sentado

43

Contrários

bem

mal

em cima

em baixo

longe

perto

frio

quente

molhado

seco

sobre

debaixo

sujo

limpo

gordo

magro

aberto

fechado

pequeno

grande

poucos

muitos

primeiro

último

à esquerda

44

fora

dentro

fácil

difícil

vazio

cheio

macio

duro

parte da frente

alto

lento

rápido

parte de trás

baixo

comprido

curto

morto

vivo

escuro

claro

velho

em cima

à direita

novo

em baixo

45

Os dias

segunda-feira

terça-feira

quarta-feira

quinta-feira

sexta-feira

sábado

domingo

o calendário

a manhã

a tarde

o sol

a noite

o espaço

a lua

a estrela

o planeta

a nave espacial

o telescópio

Dias especiais

o aniversário

o cartão de
aniversário

as férias

a vela

o presente

o bolo de aniversário

o dia do casamento

a máquina
fotográfica

a dama de honor

a noiva

o noivo

o fotógrafo

o dia de Natal

a rena

o trenó

Pai Natal

a árvore
de Natal

47

O tempo

o sol

as nuvens

o céu

o guarda-chuva

a chuva

o relâmpago

o nevoeiro

a neve

o orvalho

o vento

a neblina

a geada

o arco-íris

As estações do ano

a Primavera

o Verão

o Outono

o Inverno

Animais de estimação

a veterinária

o hámster

o porquinho-da-índia

a casota do cão

o cão

o cachorro

a comida

o periquito

o papagaio

o bico

o coelho

o canário

a gaiola

o gato

a cama do gato

o gatinho

o rato

o leite

os peixinhos dourados

49

Os desportos

o basquetebol

remar

a vela

o windsurf

o snowboarding

a raqueta

o ténis

o futebol americano

a ginástica

o críquete

o karaté

o taco

a bola

a cana de pesca

a pesca

o anzol

o râguebi

o ballet

o basebol

o mergulho

a piscina

a natação

a corrida

o tiro
ao arco

o alvo

a asa delta

a corrida

o capacete

o ciclismo

a escalada

o judo

o cavalo

o pónei

o cacifo

o futebol

a equitação

o vestiário

o badminton

os patins
de gelo

o ténis de mesa

a patinagem artística

o bastão
de esqui

o teleférico

o esqui

esquiar

o sumo

As cores

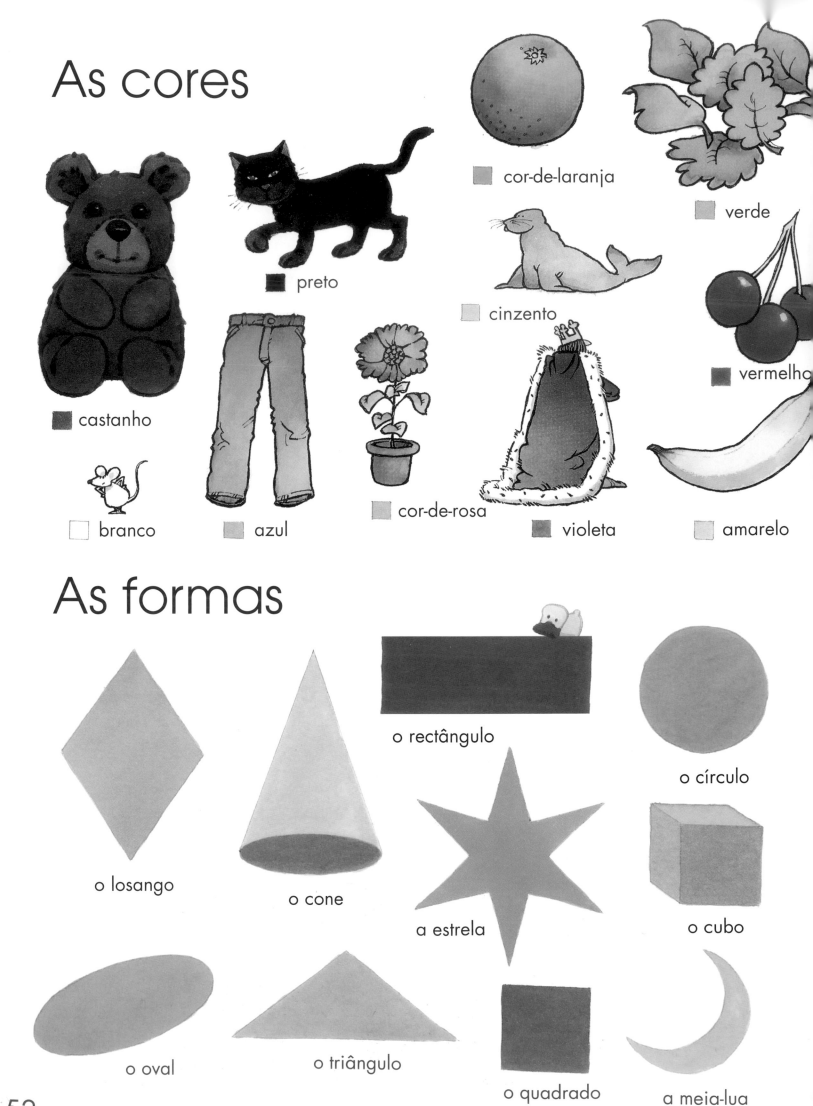

cor-de-laranja

verde

preto

cinzento

vermelho

castanho

cor-de-rosa

branco

azul

violeta

amarelo

As formas

o rectângulo

o círculo

o losango

o cone

a estrela

o cubo

o oval

o triângulo

o quadrado

a meia-lua

Os números

1	um	
2	dois	
3	três	
4	quatro	
5	cinco	
6	seis	
7	sete	
8	oito	
9	nove	
10	dez	
11	onze	
12	doze	
13	treze	
14	catorze	
15	quinze	
16	dezasseis	
17	dezassete	
18	dezoito	
19	dezanove	
20	vinte	

53

A feira popular

o carrossel

o colchão

o escorrega

a roda gigante

o comboio fantasma

as pipocas

o jogo das argolas

a montanha-russa

a barraca de tiro

os carrinhos de choque

o algodão doce

54

O circo

o equilibrista

a vara

o trapezista

a corda bamba

o monociclista

a escada de corda

a rede de segurança

os acrobatas

o director do circo

o coelho

o cão

o arco

a cartola

o malabarista

o laço

a banda

a amazona

o palhaço

Word list

In this list, you can find all the Portuguese words in the book, listed in alphabetical order. Next to each one, you can see its pronunciation (how to say it) in letters *like this*, and then its English translation.

Remember that Portuguese nouns (words for people or things) are either masculine or feminine (see page 3). In the list, each one has **o**, **a**, **os** or **as** in front of it. These all mean "the". The words with **o** are masculine, those with **a** are feminine. For plurals (more than one) you use **os** or **as**.

About Portuguese pronunciation
Read the pronunciation guide as if it were an English word, but try to remember the following points about how Portuguese words are said:

- the part of the word in bold, **like this**, is the part you stress (say more strongly)

- when you see **(l)** or **(m)** at the end of a word, say them very lightly, almost swallowing them.

- when you see **(n)** in a pronunciation, you should barely say it; say the letter that is before it through your nose, as if you had a cold

- **ow** is always pronounced as in **down**

- the Portuguese **r** is pronounced more strongly than in English, especially at the end of a word; try rolling it a little, **rrr**

- when you see **zh**, say it like the "s" in "treasure".

A

o abecedário	*oo a-bessedahrio*	alphabet
a abelha	*eh a-belya*	bee
aberto	*abairtoo*	open
a abóbora	*eh abobora*	pumpkin
as acções	*ez asoy(n)sh*	actions
os acrobatas	*ooz acrobatash*	acrobats
o actor	*oo atour*	actor
a actriz	*eh atreesh*	actress
o açúcar	*oo asukar*	sugar
o aeroporto	*oo airoportoo*	airport
a água	*eh agwah*	water
as aguarelas	*ez agwarelash*	watercolours
a águia	*eh ageeah*	eagle
o aipo	*oo eyepoo*	celery
a alcatifa	*eh alcateefah*	carpet
a aldeia	*eh aldayia*	village
a alface	*eh alfass*	lettuce
as algas	*ez algash*	seaweed
o algodão	*oo algodow(n)*	cotton (wool)
o algodão doce	*oo algodow(n) dose*	candy floss
o alho-francês	*oo alyo-fransaysh*	leek
os alientos	*ooz alimentoosh*	food
o almoço	*oo almosoo*	lunch
a almofada	*eh almofadah*	cushion, pillow
o alperce	*oo alperse*	apricot
alto	*altoo*	high, tall
o alvo	*oo alvoo*	target
amarelo	*amareloo*	yellow
a amazona	*eh amazona*	bareback rider
a ambulância	*eh amboolansia*	ambulance
a ameixa	*eh amaysha*	plum
os amortecedores	*ooz amorte-sedooresh*	buffers
o ananás	*oo ananarsh*	pineapple
a ancinho	*eh ansinyoo*	rake
andar	*andarr*	to walk
o anel	*oo anell*	ring
os animais de estimação	*ooz animy-ish de eshtimasow(n)*	pets
o aniversário	*oo aniversahrioo*	birthday
a antena de televisão	*eh antena de televizow(n)*	TV aerial
o anzol	*oo anzohl*	fish hook
apanhar	*apanyar*	to catch
as aparas de madeira	*ez aparash de madayrah*	shavings

o apito	*oo apeetoo*	whistle
o aquário	*oo akwahrioo*	aquarium
o aquecedor	*oo a-kessedoor*	radiator
o arado	*oo arahdoo*	plough
a aranha	*eh aranya*	spider
o arbusto	*oo arbooshtoo*	bush
o arco	*oo arcoo*	bow
o arco-íris	*oo arcoo-earish*	rainbow
as armações	*ez armasoy(n)sh*	antlers
o armário	*oo armahrioo*	cupboard
o arroz	*oo arrosh*	rice
a árvore	*eh arvoreh*	tree
a árvore de Natal	*eh arvoreh de natahl*	Christmas tree
as árvores	*ez arvoresh*	trees
a asa	*eh ahza*	wing
a asa delta	*eh ahza delta*	hang-glider
o aspersor de rega	*oo ashpehrsor de rayga*	sprinkler
o aspirador	*oo ashpiradoor*	vacuum cleaner
o astronauta	*oo ashtronowta*	astronaut
os astronautas	*ooz ashtronowtash*	astronauts, spacemen
o atacador	*oo atakadoor*	shoelace
o autocarro	*oo owtoocarroo*	bus
o avental	*oo aventahl*	apron
a avestruz	*eh aveshtroosh*	ostrich
o avião	*oo aveeow(n)*	plane
a avó	*eh avoh*	grandmother
o avô	*oo avoo*	grandfather
azul	*azool*	blue
os azulejos	*ooz azoolezhoosh*	tiles

B

o badminton	*oo badmeenton*	badminton
a bailarina	*eh bye-lareena*	dancer (woman)
o bailarino	*oo bye-lareenoo*	dancer (man)
baixo	*byeshoo*	low, short
em baixo	*em byeshoo*	below, downstairs
a balança	*eh balansa*	scales
o balão	*oo balow(n)*	balloon
o balde	*oo bahld*	bucket
a baleia	*eh balayia*	whale
o ballet	*oo balay*	ballet
os baloiços	*oozh baloysush*	swings
a banana	*eh banana*	banana
a bancada	*eh bancahda*	workbench
o banco	*oo bancoo*	stool

56

Portuguese	Pronunciation	English
o banco de jardim	oo **ban**coo de zhar**deem**	park bench
a banda	eh **ban**da	band
a bandeira	eh ban**day**ra	flag
a banheira	eh ban**yay**ra	bath
o barbante	oo bar**bant**	string
as barbatanas	ezh barba**ta**nash	flippers
a barcaça	eh bar**cass**a	barge
o barco a motor	oo **bar**coo a mo**tor**	motorboat
o barco a remos	oo **bar**coo a **re**mush	rowing boat
o barco à vela	oo **bar**coo a **ve**lah	sailing boat
barraca de tiro	eh ba**ra**ca de **tee**roo	rifle range
o barracão	oo barra**cow(n)**	shed
o barril	oo bar**reel**	barrel
o basebol	oo bass**boll**	baseball
o basquetebol	oo basket**boll**	basketball
o bastão de esqui	oo bash**tow(n)** de esh**kee**	ski pole
as batatas	ezh ba**ta**tash	potatoes
as batatas fritas	ezh ba**ta**tash **free**tash	chips, crisps
a bateria	eh ba-te**ree**a	battery
o bebé	oo be**bay**	baby
beber	be**ber**	to drink
bem	**bey(m)**	good
a bengala	eh ben**gah**la	walking stick
os berlindes	oozh ber**lindsh**	marbles
o bezerro	oo be**zer**roo	calf
a bicicleta	eh beesee-**cle**ta	bicycle
o bico	oo **bee**coo	beak
o bisonte	oo bee**zont**	bison
o blusão	oo blue**zow(n)**	jacket
a boca	eh **bo**ca	mouth
a bochecha	eh bo**she**sha	cheek
os boiões	oozh boy**oy(n)sh**	jars
a bola	eh **boh**la	ball
a bolacha	eh bo**la**sha	biscuit
o bolo	oo **boh**loo	cake
o bolo de aniversário	oo **boh**loo de aniver**sah**rioo	birthday cake
os bolsos	oozh **bol**soosh	pockets
a bomba de gasolina	eh **bom**ba de gazo**lee**na	petrol pump
o bombeiro	oo bom**bay**roo	fireman
o boné	oo bo**nay**	cap
as bonecas	ezh bon**e**cush	dolls
a borboleta	eh borbo**le**ta	butterfly
a borboleta nocturna	eh borbo**le**ta no**tur**na	moth
a borracha	eh bur**ra**sha	rubber
o botão	oo bu**tow(n)**	button
as botas	ezh **boh**tash	boots
o braço	oo **bra**soo	arm
branco	**bran**coo	white
os brinquedos	oozh brin**kay**doosh	toys
a broca	eh **bro**ca	drill
o bule	oo **bool**	teapot
o buraco	oo boo**ra**coo	hole
o burro	oo **bur**roo	donkey

C

Portuguese	Pronunciation	English
a cabeça	eh ca**bes**sa	head
o cabeleireiro	oo cabelay-**ray**roo	hairdresser
o cabelo	oo ca**beh**loo	hair
o cabide	oo ca**beed**	coat rack
a cabra	eh **cab**rah	goat
as caçarolas	esh cassa**ro**lash	pans
o cachecol	oo cashe**col**	scarf
o cachorro	oo ca**shor**roo	puppy
o cacifo	oo cas**see**foo	locker
a cadeira	eh ca**day**ra	chair
a cadeira de bebé	eh ca**day**ra de be**bay**	pushchair
a cadeira de praia	eh ca**day**ra de **pry**ah	deckchair
a cadeira de rodas	eh ca**day**ra de **ro**dush	wheelchair
o caderno	oo ca**dair**noo	notebook
o café	oo ca**fay**	café
cair	ca-**eer**	to fall
o cais	oo **kye**sh	platform
a caixa	eh **kye**-sha	box, checkout
a caixa de areia	eh **kye**-sha de a**ray**ia	sandpit
a caixa de ferramentas	eh **kye**-sha de ferra**men**tash	toolbox
a caixa de fósforos	eh **kye**-sha de **fosh**-forosh	matchbox
o caixote do lixo	oo kye-**shot** do **lee**shoo	rubbish bin
as calças	esh **cal**sesh	trousers
as calças de ganga	esh **cal**sesh de **gang**a	jeans
os calções	oosh cal**soy(n)sh**	shorts
o calendário	oo calen**dah**rio	calendar
a cama	eh **ca**ma	bed
a cama do gato	eh **ca**ma do **ga**too	(cat's) basket
o camião	oo cami**ow(n)**	lorry
o camião-cisterna	oo cami**ow(n)**-sish**tair**na	tanker
o caminho	oo ca**mee**nyoo	path
o/a camionista	oo/eh camio**neesh**ta	lorry driver
a camisa	eh ca**mee**za	shirt
a camisa de dormir	eh ca**mee**za de dor**meer**	nightdress
a camisola	eh camee**zoh**la	sweatshirt
a camisola interior	eh camee**zoh**la een**ter**yor	vest
o campo	oo **cam**poo	country, field
a cana de pesca	eh **ca**na de **pesh**ka	fishing rod
o canal	oo ca**nahl**	canal
o canário	oo ca**nah**rioo	canary
o candeeiro	oo candy-**ay**roo	lamp
o candeeiro de rua	oo candy-**ay**roo de **roo**-ah	streetlamp
a caneta	eh ca**ne**ta	pen
o canguru	oo kanga**roo**	kangaroo
o canivete	oo cani**vett**	penknife
a canoa	oo ca**noah**	canoe
os canos	oosh ca**noosh**	pipes
cantar	can**tahr**	to sing
o canteiro	oo can**tay**roo	flower bed
o cantor	oo can**tour**	singer (man)
a cantora	eh can**tour**a	singer (woman)
o cão	oo **cow(n)**	dog
o cão pastor	oo **cow(n)** pash**tour**	sheepdog
o capacete	oo capa**sett**	helmet

o capô	oo *capoh*	bonnet (of car)	os cereais	oosh seri-*eye*ish	cereal
a cara	eh *cah*ra	face	a cereja	eh se*reh*zha	cherry
o caracol	oo cara*coll*	snail	o cesto	oo *sesh*too	basket
o caranguejo	oo caran*gay*zhoo	crab	o cesto de	oo *sesh*too de	waste paper
a caravana	eh cara*va*na	caravan	papéis	pa*pay*ish	basket
a carne	eh *carn*	meat	o céu	oo *say*oo	sky
o carpinteiro	oo carpin*tay*roo	carpenter	o chá	oo *shah*	tea
carregar	carre*gar*	to carry	a chaleira	eh sha*layr*a	kettle
a carrinha	eh car*ree*nya	van	a chaminé	eh shami*nay*	chimney
o carrinho de	oo car*ree*nyoo de	pram	o chão	oo *show(n)*	floor
bebé	be*bay*		o chapéu	oo sha*pay*oo	hat
o carrinho de	oo car*ree*nyoo de	trolley	o chapéu de	oo sha*pay*oo de	straw hat
compras	*com*prash		palha	*pal*ya	
o carrinho de mão	oo car*ree*nyoo de	wheelbarrow	o charco	oo *shar*coo	pond
	mow(n)		a chave	eh *shahv*	key
os carrinhos	oosh	dodgems	a chave de	eh *shahv* de	screwdriver
de choque	car*ree*nyoosh		parafusos	para*foo*zoosh	
	de *shoc*		a chave	eh *shahv*	spanner
os carris	oosh car*reesh*	railway tracks	inglesa	in*glay*za	
o carro	oo *car*roo	car	as chávenas	esh *shah*venesh	cups
o carro da	oo *car*roo da	police car	cheio	*shay*oo	full
polícia	po*lee*sia		o chocolate	oo shocu*laht*	chocolate
o carro de	oo *car*roo de	racing car	o chocolate	oo shocu*laht*	hot chocolate
corrida	cor*ree*da		quente	*kent*	
o carro dos	oo *car*roo doozh	fire engine	chorar	sho*rahr*	to cry
bombeiros	bom*bay*roosh		a chuva	eh *shoo*va	rain
a carroça	eh car*ros*sa	cart	o chuveiro	oo shoo*vay*roo	shower
o carrossel	oo carros*sel*	roundabout	o ciclismo	oo si*klizh*moo	cycling
as carruagens	esh carroo-	carriages	o cilindro	oo si*lin*droo	steam-roller
	*ah*zhens		em cima	em *see*ma	above, upstairs
o cartão de	oo car*tow(n)* de	birthday card	cinco	*sin*coo	five
aniversário	aniver*sah*rioo		o cinema	oo si*nay*ma	cinema
as cartas	esh *car*tash	letters	o cinto	oo *sin*too	belt
os cartazes	oosh car*tah*zesh	posters	cinzento	sin*zen*too	grey
o carteiro	oo car*tay*roo	postman	o circo	oo *seer*coo	circus
os cartões	oosh car*toy(n)sh*	cards	o círculo	oo *seer*cooloo	circle
ilustrados	ilush*tra*doosh		os cisnes	oosh *seezh*nesh	swans
a cartola	eh car*to*la	top hat	claro	*clah*roo	light (not dark)
a casa	eh *ca*za	house	o coelho	oo coo*ehl*yo	rabbit
a casa de banho	eh *ca*za de	bathroom	o cogumelo	oo cogoo*me*loo	mushroom
	*ban*yoo		a cola	eh *coh*lah	glue
a casa de	eh *ca*za de	doll's house	colar	coh*lar*	to stick
bonecas	bo-*ne*cash		o colar	oo coh*lar*	necklace
a casa do botão	eh *ca*za do	buttonhole	o colchão	oo col*show(n)*	mat, mattress
	bu*tow(n)*		colher	col*yair*	to pick
o casaco	oo ca*za*koo	coat	as colheres	esh col*yair*esh	spoons
o casaco de	oo ca*za*koo de	cardigan	as colheres de	esh col*yair*esh de	wooden spoons
malha	*mahl*ya		pau	*pow*	
a cascata	eh cash*kah*ta	waterfall	a colina	eh co*lee*na	hill
a casota do cão	eh ca*zo*ta do	kennel	a colmeia	eh col*may*a	beehive
	cow(n)		o comboio	oo com*boy*oo	train
a cassete	eh cas*set*	cassette tape	o comboio de	oo com*boy*oo de	goods train
a cassete de	eh cas*set* de	video tape	mercadorias	mercado*ree*ash	
vídeo	*vee*dio		o comboio	oo com*boy*oo	ghost train
castanho	cash*tan*yoo	brown	fantasma	fan*tazh*ma	
o castelo	oo cash*te*loo	castle	comer	co*mair*	to eat
o castelo de	oo cash*te*loo de	sandcastle	a comida	eh co*mee*da	food
areia	a*ray*ia		o comissário de	oo comis*sah*rio de	air steward
o castor	oo cash*tor*	beaver	bordo	*bor*doo	
catorze	ca*torze*	fourteen	a cómoda	eh *com*odah	chest of drawers
a cauda	eh *cow*da	tail	a comporta	eh com*por*ta	(canal) lock
a cavalariça	eh cavala-*ree*sa	stable	a compota	eh com*po*ta	jam
o cavalo	oo ca*va*loo	horse	comprar	com*prar*	to buy
o cavalo de	oo ca*va*loo de	rocking horse	comprido	cum*pree*doo	long
baloiço	ba*loy*soo		os comprimidos	oosh	pills
cavar	ca*var*	to dig		cumpri*mee*doosh	
o CD	oo say-*day*	CD	o computador	oo compoota*door*	computer
a cebola	eh se*bo*la	onion	a concha	eh *con*sha	shell
o celeiro	oo se*lay*roo	barn	o cone	oo *cohn*	cone
a cenoura	eh se*noo*ra	carrot	o consultório	oo consool*tor*io	surgery
a cerca	eh *sair*ka	fence	as contas	esh *con*tush	beads, sums

Portuguese	Pronunciation	English
os contrários	oosh contrahreeooosh	opposites
os copos	oosh cohpoosh	glasses (for drinking)
cor-de-laranja	cor-de-laranzha	orange (colour)
cor-de-rosa	cor-de-rohza	pink
a corda	eh corda	rope
a corda bamba	eh corda bamba	tightrope
a corda de saltar	eh corda de saltar	skipping rope
os cordeiros	oosh cordayroosh	lambs
as cores	esh corsh	colours
correr	corrair	to run
a corrida	eh correeda	jogging, race
o cortador de relva	oo cortadoor de relva	lawnmower
cortar	cortar	to cut
a cortina	eh corteena	curtain
coser	cuzair	to sew
as costas	esh coshtash	back (of body)
o cotovelo	oo cotovehloo	elbow
a couve	eh coov	cabbage
a couve-flor	eh coov-floor	cauliflower
a cozinha	eh cuzeenya	kitchen
cozinhar	cuzinyar	to cook
o cozinheiro-chefe	oo cuzinyayroo-shef	chef
as crianças	esh cree-ansash	children
o críquete	oo creeket	cricket
o crocodilo	oo crocoodeeloo	crocodile
o cubo	oo cooboo	cube
os cubos	oosh cooboosh	(toy) bricks
as cuecas	esh kwekash	pants
curto	cortoo	short

D

os dados	oozh dadoosh	dice
a dama de honor	eh dahma de onor	bridesmaid
dançar	dansar	to dance
debaixo	de-byeshoo	under
os dedos	oozh dedoosh	fingers
os dedos do pé	oozh dedoosh do peh	toes
os degraus	oozh degrowsh	steps
os dentes	oozh dentsh	teeth
o/a dentista	oo/eh dentishta	dentist
dentro	dentroo	inside
o desenho	oo dezenyoo	drawing
os desportos	oozh deshportoosh	sports
o detergente	oo deterzhent	washing powder
dez	desh	ten
dezanove	dezanov	nineteen
dezasseis	dezasaysh	sixteen
dezassete	dezasett	seventeen
dezoito	dezoytoo	eighteen
o dia de Natal	oo deea de natahl	Christmas Day
o dia do casamento	oo deea do cazamentoo	wedding day
os dias	oozh deeash	days
os dias especiais	oozh deeash eshpessi-eyeish	special days
difícil	difeesil	difficult
o dinheiro	oo dinyayroo	money
o director do circo	oo diretor do seerkoo	ringmaster
à direita	ah deerayta	right
os disfarces	oozh dishfarsesh	fancy dress
o distintivo	oo dishtinteevoo	badge
dois	doysh	two
domingo	domingoo	Sunday
dormir	doormeer	to sleep
doze	doz	twelve
o dromedário	oo dromedahrio	camel
duro	dooroo	hard

E

o edredão	oo edredow(n)	duvet
o elefante	oo elefant	elephant
o elevador	oo elevadoor	lift
a empregada	eh empregahda	waitress
o empregado	oo empregahdoo	waiter
empurrar	empoorrar	to push
a enfermeira	eh enfermayra	nurse (woman)
o enfermeiro	oo enfermayroo	nurse (man)
a entrada	eh entrahda	hall
a enxada	eh enshahda	hoe
o equilibrista	oo iki-libreeshta	tightrope walker
a equitação	eh ikitasow(n)	riding
as ervilhas	ez airveelyash	peas
a escada	eh eshkahda	ladder
a escada de corda	eh eshkahda de corda	rope ladder
as escadas	ez eshkahdash	stairs
a escalada	eh eshkalada	climbing
a escavadora	eh eshkavadoora	digger
a escola	eh eshkola	school
esconder-se	eshkondair-se	to hide
o escorrega	oo eshkorrayga	helter-skelter, slide
a escova	eh eshkova	brush
a escova de dentes	eh eshkova de dentsh	toothbrush
escrever	eshkrevair	to write
escuro	eshkooroo	dark
escutar	eshkootar	to listen
a esfregona	eh eshfregona	mop
o espaço	oo eshpassoo	space
o espantalho	oo eshpantalyo	scarecrow
o esparguete	oo eshpargett	spaghetti
o espelho	oo eshpelyo	mirror
esperar	eshperar	to wait
os espinafres	ooz eshpinafrush	spinach
a espingarda	eh eshpingarda	gun
a esponja	eh eshponzha	sponge
a esposa	eh eshpoza	wife
à esquerda	ah eshkairda	left
o esqui	oo eshkee	ski
o esqui aquático	oo eshkee akwatikoo	water-skiing
esquiar	eshkeear	to ski
o esquilo	oo eshkeeloo	squirrel
o estábulo	oo eshtabooloo	cowshed
a estação de comboio	eh eshtasow(n) de comboyoo	railway station
a estação de serviço	eh eshtasow(n) de sairveesoo	garage
as estações do ano	ez eshtasoy(n)sh do anoo	seasons
estar sentado	eshtar sentahdoo	to sit
o estômago	oo eshtohmagoo	stomach
a estrada	eh eshtrahdah	road
a estrela	eh eshtrela	star
a estrela-do-mar	eh eshtrela-do-mar	starfish
a estufa	eh eshtoofa	greenhouse
eu	yo	me

F

a fábrica	eh fabrica	factory
as facas	esh facash	knives
fácil	fassil	easy
falar	falar	to talk
a família	eh fameelia	family

Portuguese	Pronunciation	English
os fardos de palha	oosh **far**doosh de **pa**lya	straw bales
a farinha	eh fa**ree**nya	flour
os faróis	oosh fa**roysh**	headlamps
o farol	oo fa**rol**	lighthouse
o fato de banho	oo **fa**too de **ba**nyoo	swimsuit
fazer malha	fa**zair ma**lya	to knit
fechado	fe**shah**doo	closed
o fecho de correr	oo **fesh**oo de cor**rair**	zip
o feijão verde	oo fay**zhow(n) vaird**	green beans
a feira popular	eh **fay**ra popoo**lar**	fairground
o feno	oo **feh**noo	hay
as férias	esh **fair**iash	holidays
o ferro-de-engomar	oo **fer**roo-de-engo**mar**	iron
a festa	eh **fesh**ta	party
a filha	eh **fee**lya	daughter
o filho	oo **fee**lyoo	son
os filhotes de leão	oosh fee**lyotsh** de lee**ow(n)**	lion cubs
a fita métrica	eh **fee**ta **me**trica	measuring tape
a fivela	eh fee**ve**la	buckle
a flauta	eh **flow**ta	flute, recorder
as flechas	esh **fle**shash	arrows
as flores	esh **floor**sh	flowers
a floresta	eh flo**resh**ta	forest
a foca	eh **fo**ca	seal
o fogão	oo fo**gow(n)**	stove
a fogueira	eh fo**gay**ra	bonfire
o foguetão	oo fo-ge**tow(n)**	rocket
os foguetes	oosh fo**getsh**	fireworks
as folhas	esh **fo**lyash	leaves
fora	**fo**ra	outside
as formas	esh **for**mash	shapes
a forquilha	eh for**kee**lya	garden fork
os fósforos	oosh **fosh**foroosh	matches
as fotografias	esh fotogra**fee**-esh	photos
o fotógrafo	oo fo**to**grafoo	photographer
a fralda	eh **fral**da	nappy
a framboesa	eh frambo**ay**za	raspberry
o frango	oo **fran**goo	chicken
a frigideira	eh frizhi**day**ra	frying pan
o frigorífico	oo frigo**ri**ficoo	fridge
frio	**free**oo	cold
as frutas	esh **froo**tash	fruit
o fumo	oo **foo**moo	smoke
o futebol	oo foot**boll**	football
o futebol americano	oo foot**boll** ameri**ca**noo	American football

G

Portuguese	Pronunciation	English
a gaiola	eh guy**o**la	cage
a gaivota	eh guy**vo**ta	seagull
as galinhas	ezh ga**lee**nyash	hens
o galinheiro	oo gali**nyay**roo	henhouse
o galo	oo **ga**loo	cockerel
os gansos	oozh **gan**soosh	geese
os garfos	oozh **gar**foosh	forks
as garrafas	ezh gar**ra**fash	bottles
a gasolina	eh gazo**lee**na	petrol
gatinhar	gatin**yar**	to crawl
o gatinho	oo ga**tee**nyo	kitten
o gato	oo **ga**too	cat
a gaveta	eh ga**ve**ta	drawer
a geada	eh zhe**ah**da	frost
o gelado	oo zhe**lah**doo	ice cream
o gesso	oo **zhes**soo	plaster
a ginástica	eh zhee**nash**tica	gym

Portuguese	Pronunciation	English
a girafa	eh zhee**ra**fa	giraffe
os girinos	oosh zhee**ree**noosh	tadpoles
o giz	oo **zheesh**	chalk
o globo terrestre	oo **gloh**boo ter**resh**tre	globe
o golfinho	oo gol**fee**nyoo	dolphin
gordo	**gor**doo	fat
o gorila	oo go**ree**la	gorilla
grande	**grand**	big
a gravata	eh gra**va**ta	tie
a grinalda de papel	eh gri**nal**da de pa**pell**	paper chain
a grua	eh **groo**a	crane
o guarda-chuva	oo **gwar**da-**shoo**va	umbrella
o guarda-roupa	oo **gwar**da-**roh**pa	wardrobe
o guarda-sol	oo **gwar**da-**sol**	beach umbrella
a guitarra	eh gee**tar**ra	guitar

H

Portuguese	Pronunciation	English
o hambúrger	oo am**bor**ger	hamburger
o hámster	oo **am**shtair	hamster
a harmónica	eh ar**mo**nica	harmonica
o helicóptero	oo eli**cop**teroo	helicopter
o hipopótamo	oo ipo**po**tamoo	hippopotamus
o homem	oo **oh**me(m)	man
a hospedeira	eh oshpe**day**ra	stewardess
o hospital	oo oshpee**tal**	hospital
o hotel	oo oh**tel**	hotel

I

Portuguese	Pronunciation	English
o icebergue	oo eis-**bairg**	iceberg
a ilha	eh **eel**ya	island
o interruptor	oo interrup**tor**	switch
o Inverno	oo in**vair**noo	winter
o iogurte	oo yo**gort**	yoghurt
a irmã	eh eer**ma(n)**	sister
o irmão	oo eer**mow(n)**	brother

J

Portuguese	Pronunciation	English
a janela	eh zha**ne**la	window
o jantar	oo zhan**tar**	dinner, supper
o jardim	oo zhar**deem**	garden
o jardim zoológico	oo zhar**deem** zo-o**lo**zhicoo	zoo
a joaninha	eh zhoa**nee**nha	ladybird
o joelho	oo zho-**ehl**yo	knee
jogar	zho**gar**	to play
o jogo das argolas	oo **zho**goo des ar**go**lash	hoop-la
o jornal	oo **zhor**nal	newspaper
o judo	oo **zhoo**doo	judo
o juiz	oo zhoo**eesh**	judge

K

Portuguese	Pronunciation	English
o karaté	oo kara**teh**	karate

L

Portuguese	Pronunciation	English
os lábios	oozh **la**bioosh	lips
o laço	oo **la**soo	bow tie, ribbon
a lagarta	eh la**gar**ta	caterpillar
o lagarto	oo la**gar**too	lizard
o lago	oo **lah**goo	lake
a lama	eh **lah**ma	mud
a lâmpada	eh **lam**pada	light bulb
lançar	lan**sar**	to throw
o lápis	oo **la**pish	pencil
os lápis de cera	oozh **la**pis de **seh**ra	crayons

a laranja	eh la*ran*zha	orange (fruit)
a lata de tinta	eh **la**ta de **teen**ta	paint pot
as latas de conservas	ezh **la**tash de con**sair**vash	tins
a lavagem automática	eh la**vah**zhem auto**ma**tica	car wash
o lava-louça	oo **la**va-**loy**sa	sink
lavar-se	**la**var-se	to wash
o lavatório	oo lava**to**rioo	washbasin
o lavrador	oo lavra**door**	farmer
o leão	oo lee**ow(n)**	lion
os legumes	oozh le**goo**mesh	vegetables
o leite	oo **layt**	milk
os leitões	oozh lay**toy(n)sh**	piglets
o lenço	oo **len**soo	handkerchief
o lençol	oo len**soll**	sheet
os lenços de papel	oozh **len**soosh de pa**pell**	tissues
a lenha	eh **le**nya	logs
lento	**len**too	slow
o leopardo	oo lioo**par**doo	leopard
ler	**lair**	to read
a ligadura	eh liga**door**a	bandage
a lima	eh **lee**ma	file
o limão	oo li**mow(n)**	lemon
limpo	**leem**poo	clean
a língua	eh **leeng**wa	tongue
os livros	oozh **leev**roosh	books
a lixa	eh **lee**sha	sandpaper
o lixo	oo **lee**shoo	rubbish
o lobo	oo **loh**boh	wolf
a locomotiva	eh locomo**tee**va	(train) engine
a loja	eh **lo**zha	shop
a loja de brinquedos	eh **lo**zha de brin**kay**doosh	toyshop
longe	**lonzh**	far
o losango	oo lu**zang**oo	diamond (shape)
a lua	eh **loo**ah	moon
lutar	loo**tar**	to fight
as luvas	ezh **loo**vash	gloves

M

a maçã	eh ma**sa(n)**	apple
o macaco	oo ma**ca**coo	monkey
o machado	oo ma**shah**doo	axe
macio	ma**see**oo	soft
a madeira	eh ma**day**ra	wood
a mãe	eh **my(n)**	mother
magro	**ma**groo	thin
mal	**mah(l)**	bad
a mala	eh **mah**la	handbag, suitcase
o malabarista	oo malaba**reesh**ta	juggler
a mangueira	eh man**gay**ra	hosepipe
a manhã	eh ma**nya(n)**	morning
a manteiga	eh man**tay**ga	butter
a mão	eh **mow(n)**	hand
o mapa	oo **ma**pa	map
a máquina de bilhetes	eh **ma**kina de bi**lyetsh**	ticket machine
a máquina de lavar roupa	eh **ma**kina de la**var roh**pa	washing machine
a máquina fotográfica	eh **ma**kina foto**gra**fica	camera
o maquinista	oo maki**neesh**ta	train driver
o mar	oo **mar**	sea
os marcadores	oozh marca**door**esh	felt tips
o marido	oo ma**ree**doo	husband
o marinheiro	oo marin**yay**roo	sailor
as marionetas	ezh mario**ne**tash	puppets
o martelo	oo mar**te**loo	hammer

o martelo pneumático	oo mar**te**loo p'nayoo**ma**ticoo	pneumatic drill
as máscaras	ezh **mash**carash	masks
o mealheiro	oo mia**lyay**roo	money box
a mecânica	eh me**ca**nica	mechanic(woman)
o mecânico	oo me**ca**nicoo	mechanic (man)
a meda de feno	eh **meh**da de **feh**noo	haystack
a médica	eh **me**dica	doctor (woman)
o médico	oo **me**dicoo	doctor (man)
o medicamento	oo medica**men**too	medicine
a meia-lua	eh **may**a-**loo**ah	crescent
as meias	ezh **may**esh	socks
as meias-calças	esh **may**esh-**cal**sash	tights
o mel	oo **mell**	honey
o melão	oo me**low(n)**	melon
a menina	eh me**nee**na	girl
o menino	oo me**nee**noo	boy
o mercado	oo mer**cah**doo	market
o mergulhador	oo mergoolya**door**	frogman
o mergulho	oo mer**goo**lyoo	diving
a mesa	eh **me**za	table
a minhoca	eh mi**nyo**ca	worm
a mochila	eh mo**shee**la	backpack
o mocho	oo **mo**shoo	owl
o moinho de vento	oo mo**een**yoo de **ven**too	windmill
molhado	mo**lyah**doo	wet
o molho de tomate	oo **mo**lyo de to**matt**	ketchup
o monociclista	oo monosi**cleesh**ta	trick cyclist
a montanha	eh mon**tan**ya	mountain
a montanha-russa	eh mon**tan**ya-**roos**sa	big dipper
o morango	oo mo**rang**oo	strawberry
o morcego	oo mor**say**goo	bat
morto	**mor**too	dead
a mosca	eh **mosh**ka	fly
a moto	eh **moh**toh	motorbike
o motor	oo moh**tor**	(car) engine
o motorista de autocarro	oo moto**reesh**ta de owtoo**car**roo	bus driver
muitos	**mween**toosh	many
as muletas	ezh moo**le**tash	crutches
a mulher	eh moo**lyair**	woman
a mulher-polícia	eh moo**lyair**-pu**lee**sia	policewoman

N

o nariz	oo na**reesh**	nose
a natação	eh nata**sow(n)**	swimming
as natas	ezh **na**tash	cream
a nave espacial	eh nav eshpas**sial**	spaceship
o navio	oo na**vee**-oo	ship
a neblina	eh ne**blee**na	mist
a neve	eh **nev**	snow
o nevoeiro	oo nevo**ay**roo	fog
o ninho	oo **neen**yoo	nest
a noite	eh **noyt**	night
a noiva	eh **noy**va	bride
o noivo	oo **noy**voo	bridegroom
nove	**nov**	nine
novo	**noh**voo	new
os números	oozh **noo**meroosh	numbers
as nuvens	ezh **noo**vensh	clouds

O

a oficina	eh ofi**see**na	workshop
oito	**oy**too	eight
o óleo	oo **oh**lioo	oil

Portuguese	Pronunciation	English
o olho	oo *olyoo*	eye
os ombros	ooz *om*broosh	shoulders
a omeleta	eh oma*le*ta	omelette
as ondas	ez *on*dush	waves
onze	*onz*	eleven
as orelhas	ez o*reh*lyash	ears
o orvalho	oo or*val*yoo	dew
o osso	oo *os*soo	bone
o ouriço-cacheiro	oo ooree*soo*-ca*shay*roo	hedgehog
o Outono	oo oo*ton*oo	autumn
o oval	oo oh*vall*	oval
as ovelhas	ez oh*vel*yash	sheep
o ovo estrelado	oo *o*voo eshtre*lah*doo	fried egg
o ovo quente	oo *o*voo **kent**	boiled egg
os ovos	ooz *o*voosh	eggs

P

a pá	eh **pah**	spade, trowel
a pá do lixo	eh **pah** do **lee**shoo	dustpan
a padeira	eh pa*day*rah	baker (woman)
o padeiro	oo pa*day*roo	baker (man)
os pãezinhos	oosh pie(n)-*zee*nyoosh	bread rolls
o pai	oo **pie**	father
o Pai Natal	oo **pie** na*tahl*	Father Christmas
o palhaço	oo pa*lya*soo	clown
o palheiro	oo pa*lyay*roo	hayloft
a palhinha	eh pa*lyee*nya	(drinking) straw
o panda	oo **pan**da	panda
o pano de cozinha	oo **pan**oo de cu*zee*nya	tea towel
o pano do pó	oo **pan**oo do **poh**	duster
as panquecas	esh pan*ke*kash	pancakes
as pantufas	esh pan*too*fash	slippers
o pão	oo **pow(n)**	bread
o papagaio	oo papa*guy*oo	parrot
o papagaio de papel	oo papa*guy*oo de pa*pell*	kite
o papel	oo pa*pell*	paper
o papel higiénico	oo pa*pell* eezhye*nicoo*	toilet paper
o pára-quedas	oo para-*kay*dush	parachute
os parafusos	oosh para*foo*zush	screws
os parafusos de porca	oosh para*foo*zush de **por**ca	bolts
a parede	eh pa*rade*	wall
o parque	oo **park**	park
a parte da frente	eh **part** da **frent**	front
a parte de trás	eh **part** de **trarsh**	back (not front)
partir	par*tier*	to break
a passadeira de peões	eh passa*day*ra de pi*oy(n)sh*	crossing
os pássaros	oosh **passa**roosh	birds
o passeio	oo passa*yoo*	pavement
a pasta de dentes	eh **pash**ta de **dentsh**	toothpaste
o pastor	oo pash*toor*	shepherd
a pastora	eh pash*toora*	shepherdess
as patas	esh **pa**tash	paws
a patinagem artística	eh pati*nahzhem* ar*tish*tica	ice skating
os patinhos	oosh pa*tee*nyoosh	ducklings
os patins	oosh pa*teensh*	roller blades
os patins de gelo	oosh pa*teensh* de **zhe**loo	ice skates
os patos	oosh pa*toosh*	ducks
os paus	oosh **powsh**	sticks
os pauzinhos	oosh pow*zee*nyoosh	chopsticks

Portuguese	Pronunciation	English
o pé	oo **peh**	foot
os pedaços de madeira	oosh peda*soosh* de ma*day*ra	(bits of) wood
as pedras	esh **pe**drash	stones
pegar	pe*gar*	to take
o peito	oo **pay**too	chest
o peixe	oo **paysh**	fish
os peixinhos dourados	oosh pay*shee*nyoosh du*rah*doosh	goldfish
o pelicano	oo peli*cah*noo	pelican
as penas	esh **pen**ash	feathers
o penhasco	oo pe*nyash*coo	cliff
pensar	pen*sar*	to think
o penso-rápido	oo **pen**soo-*ra*pidoo	sticking plaster
o pente	oo **pent**	comb
o pepino	oo pe*pee*noo	cucumber
pequeno	pe*ke*noo	small
o pequeno-almoço	oo pe*ke*noo-al*mos*soo	breakfast
a pêra	eh **pai**ra	pear
o periquito	oo peri*kee*too	budgerigar
a perna	eh **pair**na	leg
a persiana	eh pairsee*ah*na	blind (for a window)
perto	**pair**too	near
os perus	oosh pe*roosh*	turkeys
a pesca	eh **pesh**ka	fishing
o pescador	oo peshka*door*	fisherman
o pescoço	oo pesh*kos*soo	neck
o pêssego	oo **pes**segoo	peach
o petroleiro	oo petro*lay*roo	oil tanker
o piano	oo pi*ah*noo	piano
o pijama	oo pi*zha*ma	pyjamas
o piloto	oo pi*lo*too	pilot
a pimenta	eh pi*men*ta	pepper
o pincel	oo pin*sell*	paintbrush
o pinguim	oo pin*gwee(m)*	penguin
os pintainhos	oosh pinta-*ee*nyoosh	chicks
pintar	pin*tar*	to paint
o pintor	oo pin*toor*	painter (man)
a pintora	eh pin*toora*	painter (woman)
as pinturas para a cara	esh pin*toor*ash **pa**ra eh **cah**ra	face paints
as pipocas	esh pi*po*cash	popcorn
o piquenique	oo peek*neek*	picnic
os pires	oosh **pi**resh	saucers
a piscina	eh pish*see*na	swimming pool
a pista de aterragem	eh **pish**ta de ater*rah*zhem	runway
a pizza	eh **peet**sa	pizza
a plaina	eh **ply**ena	(shaving) plane
o planeta	oo pla*ne*ta	planet
a planta	eh **plan**ta	plant
a plasticina	eh plashti*see*na	modelling clay
o pneu	oo p'*nay*oo	tyre
a poça de água	eh **pos**sa de **ag**wa	puddle
a pocilga	eh pos*sil*ga	pigsty
o polegar	oo po-le*gar*	thumb
a polícia	oo po*lee*sia	policeman
o pomar	oo po*mar*	orchard
o pombo	oo **pom**boo	pigeon
o pónei	oo **poh**nay	pony
a ponte	eh **pont**	bridge
as porcas	esh **por**cash	nuts (for bolts)
os porcos	oosh **por**coosh	pigs
o porquinho-da-índia	oo por*kee*nyoo-da-*een*dia	guinea pig
a porta	eh **por**ta	door

Portuguese	Pronunciation	English
o porta-bagagens	oo **porta**-ba**ga**zhens	boot (of car)
o porta-moedas	oo **porta**-mo**ay**dush	purse
o portão	oo por**tow(n)**	gate
o poste sinalizador	oo **posht** sinaleeza**door**	signpost
poucos	**poh**cush	few
a praia	eh **pry**ia	beach
os pratos	oosh **prah**toosh	plates
o prédio	oo **pre**dio	block of flats
os pregos	oosh **pre**goosh	nails
as prendas	esh **pren**dash	presents
o presente	oo pre**zent**	present
o presunto	oo pre**zoon**too	ham
preto	**pre**too	black
a Primavera	eh preema**vay**ra	spring
o primeiro	oo pree**may**roo	first
o primo	oo **pree**moo	cousin
o professor	oo profes**soor**	teacher (man)
a professora	eh profes**soor**a	teacher (woman)
as profissões	esh profis**soy(n)sh**	jobs
o pulôver	oo pu**loh**ver	jumper
o puré de batata	oo poo**ray** de ba**ta**ta	mashed potatoes
o puxador	oo poosha**door**	door handle
puxar	poo**shar**	to pull
o puzzle	oo **pah**zel	jigsaw puzzle

Q

Portuguese	Pronunciation	English
o quadrado	oo kwa**drah**doo	square
o quadro	oo **kwad**roo	picture
o quadro preto	oo **kwad**roo **pre**too	blackboard
quarta-feira	**kwar**ta-**fay**ra	Wednesday
o quarto	oo **kwar**too	bedroom
quatro	**kwa**troo	four
o queijo	oo **kay**zhoo	cheese
o queixo	oo **kay**shoo	chin
quente	**kent**	hot
a quinta	eh **keen**ta	farm, farmhouse
quinta-feira	**keen**ta-fayra	Thursday
quinze	**keenz**	fifteen

R

Portuguese	Pronunciation	English
a rã	eh **ra(n)**	frog
o rabinho	oo ra**bee**nyoo	bottom (of body)
rachar	ra**shar**	to chop
o rádio	oo **rah**dio	radio
o râguebi	oo **rag**bee	rugby
rápido	**ra**pidoo	fast
a raposa	eh ra**poh**za	fox (female)
as raposinhas	ezh ra**poh**zee**ny**ash	fox cubs
a raqueta	eh ra**ke**ta	racket
o rato	oo **ra**too	mouse
o reboque	oo re**bok**	breakdown lorry
o rebuçado	oo re**boo**sah**doo**	sweet
o recreio	oo re**cray**oo	playground
o rectângulo	oo re**tang**ooloo	rectangle
a rede	eh **red**	net
a rede de segurança	eh **red** de segoo**ran**sa	safety net
o regador	oo rega**door**	watering can
o regato	oo re**ga**too	stream
a régua	eh **reg**wa	ruler
o relâmpago	oo re**lam**pagoo	lightning
o relógio	oo re**lo**zhioo	clock, watch
a relva	eh **rel**va	grass
remar	re**mar**	rowing (racing)
o remo	oo **re**moo	oar
o remo de canoa	oo **re**moo de ca**noh**-a	paddle
a rena	eh **reh**na	reindeer
o revisor	oo revee**zoor**	ticket inspector (man)
a revisora	eh revee**zoor**a	ticket inspector (woman)
a revista	eh re**veesh**ta	magazine
o rinoceronte	oo rinosse**ront**	rhinoceros
o rio	oo **ree**-oo	river
rir	**reer**	to laugh
o robot	oo ro**boh**	robot
os rochedos	oozh ro**shay**doosh	rocks
a roda	eh **roh**da	wheel
a roda gigante	eh **roh**da zhee**gant**	big wheel
a roupa	eh **roh**pa	clothes
o roupão	oo roh**pow(n)**	dressing gown
a rua	eh **roo**-a	street

S

Portuguese	Pronunciation	English
sábado	**sa**–badoo	Saturday
o sabonete	oo sabo**nett**	soap
o saco	oo **sa**coo	bag
a saia	eh **sye**-a	skirt
o sal	oo **sal**	salt
a sala de espera	eh **sah**la de esh**pe**ra	waiting room
a sala de estar	eh **sah**la de esh**tar**	living room
a salada	eh sa**la**da	salad
o salame	oo sa**lahm**e	salami
a salsicha	eh sal**see**sha	sausage
saltar	sal**tar**	to jump
saltar à corda	sal**tar** a **cor**da	to skip
as sandálias	esh san**dahl**iash	sandals
a sanduíche	eh sand**weech**	sandwich
a sanita	eh sa**nee**ta	toilet
os sapatos	oosh sa**pah**toosh	shoes
os sapatos de ténis	oosh sa**pah**toosh de **te**nish	trainers
o sapo	oo **sa**poo	toad
a sebe	eh **seb**	hedge
seco	**se**coo	dry
a secretária	eh secre**tah**ria	desk
segunda-feira	se**goon**da-**fay**ra	Monday
seis	**saysh**	six
os seixos	oosh **say**shoosh	pebbles
a sela	eh **seh**la	saddle
o semáforo	oo se**ma**foroo	traffic lights
as sementes	esh se**mentsh**	seeds
a seringa	eh si**ring**a	syringe
a serpente	eh ser**pent**	snake
a serra	eh **serr**a	saw
a serradura	eh serra**door**a	sawdust
sete	**set**	seven
sexta-feira	**sesh**ta-**fay**ra	Friday
os sinais	oosh si**nye**-ish	signals
o skate	oo **skait**	skateboard
o snowboarding	oo sno**bord**ing	snowboarding
o sobe e desce	oo **sob** ee **desh**se	seesaw
a sobrancelha	eh sobran-**sehl**ya	eyebrow
sobre	**sob**reh	on
as sobremesas	esh sobre**mehz**ash	puddings
o sofá	oo so**fah**	sofa
o sol	oo **sol**	sun
os soldadinhos de chumbo	oosh solda**dee**nyoosh de **shoom**boo	toy soldiers
a sopa	eh **so**pa	soup

soprar	*soprar*	to blow
sorrir	*surrir*	to smile
o submarino	*oo soobmareenoo*	submarine
sujo	*soozhoo*	dirty
o sumo	*oo soomoo*	juice, sumo wrestling
o supermercado	*oo sooper-mercahdoo*	supermarket

T

a T-shirt	*eh tee-shirt*	T-shirt
a tábua	*eh tabooa*	plank
a tábua de passar a ferro	*eh tabooa de passar a ferroo*	ironing board
o tabuleiro	*oo taboolayroo*	tray
as taças	*esh tasash*	bowls, dishes
as tachas	*esh tashash*	tacks, drawing pins
o taco	*oo tacoo*	bat (for sports)
o talhante	*oo talyant*	butcher
os tambores	*oosh tambor-esh*	drums
a tangerina	*eh tanzhereena*	tangerine
o tapete	*oo tapett*	rug
a tarde	*eh tard*	afternoon
a tartaruga	*eh tartarooga*	tortoise
o táxi	*oo taksi*	taxi
o tecto	*oo tetoo*	ceiling
a teia de aranha	*eh tayia de aranya*	spider's web
o teleférico	*oo telyfehricoo*	chairlift
o telefone	*oo telyfon*	telephone
o telescópio	*oo telyshkopioo*	telescope
a televisão	*eh telyvizow(n)*	television
o telhado	*oo telyahdoo*	roof
o tempo	*oo tempoo*	weather
as tendas de campismo	*esh tendash de campeezhmoo*	tents
o ténis	*oo tehnish*	tennis
o ténis de mesa	*oo tehnish de meza*	table tennis
terça-feira	*tairsa-fayra*	Tuesday
o termómetro	*oo tairmometro*	thermometer
a terra	*eh terra*	earth
a tesoura	*eh tezoora*	scissors
o texugo	*oo teshoogoo*	badger
a tia	*eh tee-a*	aunt
o tigre	*oo teegra*	tiger
os tijolos	*oosh tizhohloosh*	bricks
as tintas	*esh teentash*	paints
o tio	*oo teeoo*	uncle
o tiro ao arco	*oo teeroo ow arcoo*	archery
a toalha	*eh to-ahlya*	towel
a toalha de mesa	*eh to-ahlya de meza*	tablecloth
o tomate	*oo tomat*	tomato
a toranja	*eh toranzha*	grapefruit
a torneira	*eh tornayra*	tap
o torno de bancada	*oo tornoo de bancahda*	vice

as torradas	*esh torrahdash*	toast
a torre de controlo	*eh torreh de controhloo*	control tower
a toupeira	*eh toopayra*	mole
o touro	*oo touroo*	bull
o tractor	*oo tratoor*	tractor
a traineira	*eh trynayra*	fishing boat
a trapezista	*eh trapezeeshta*	trapeze artist
a trela	*eh trehla*	(dog) lead
o trenó	*oo trenoh*	sleigh
trepar	*trepar*	to climb
três	*traysh*	three
treze	*trayze*	thirteen
o triângulo	*oo treeangooloo*	triangle
o triciclo	*oo treeseecloo*	tricycle
a tromba	*eh tromba*	trunk
a trombeta	*eh trombeta*	trumpet
o tubarão	*oo toobarrow(n)*	shark
o túnel	*oo toonel*	tunnel

U

o último	*oo ulteemoo*	last
um	*oom*	one
o urso	*oo orsoo*	bear
o urso de peluche	*oo orsoo de peloosh*	teddy bear
o urso polar	*oo orsoo polar*	polar bear
as uvas	*ez oovash*	grapes

V

a vaca	*eh vaca*	cow
a vara	*eh vahra*	perch, pole
varrer	*varrair*	to sweep
a vassoura	*eh vassoora*	broom
vazio	*vazeeoo*	empty
o veado	*oo vi-ahdoo*	deer
a vela	*eh vehla*	candle, sailing
velho	*vehlyo*	old
o vento	*oo ventoo*	wind
ver	*vair*	to see, to watch
o Verão	*oo vurow(n)*	summer
verde	*verd*	green
vermelho	*vermehlyoo*	red
a vespa	*eh veshpa*	wasp
o vestiário	*oo veshtiahrio*	changing room
o vestido	*oo veshteedoo*	dress
a veterinária	*eh veterinahria*	vet (woman)
o veterinário	*oo veterinahrioo*	vet (man)
as viagens	*ezh veeahzhens*	travel
vinte	*vint*	twenty
violeta	*veeoleta*	purple
vivo	*veevoo*	alive

W

o windsurf	*oo weendsarfe*	windsurfing

Z

a zebra	*eh zehbra*	zebra

First published in 2007 by Usborne Publishing Ltd, Usborne House, 83-85 Saffron Hill, London EC1N 8RT, England. www.usborne.com